Of Grave Dirt and Stardust.

Cassandra Griffin

BookLeaf Publishing

Presentation by *BookLeaf Publishing*

Web: www.bookleafpub.com

E-mail: info@bookleafpub.com

ISBN: 9789357616423

First edition 2022

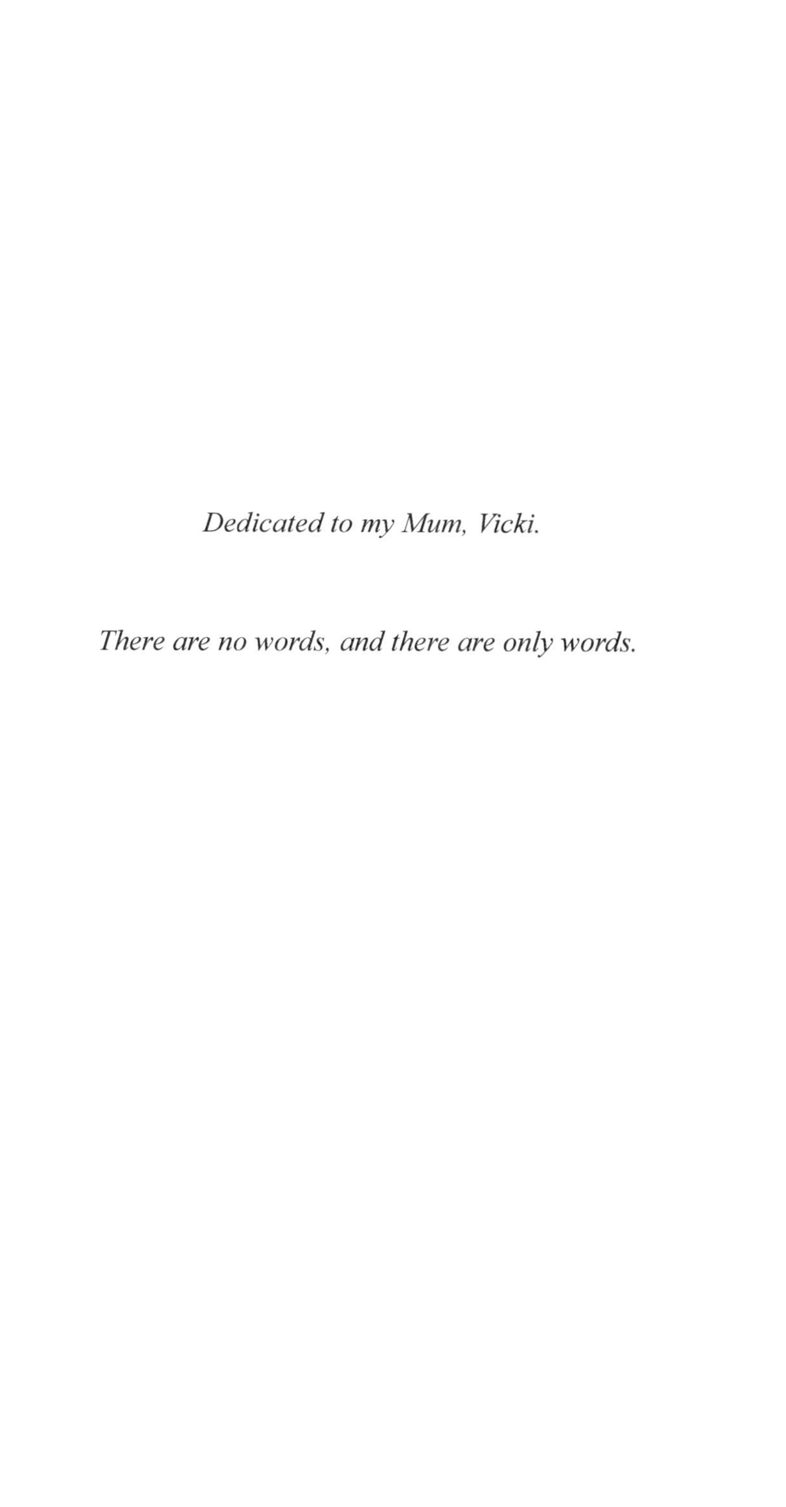

Dedicated to my Mum, Vicki.

There are no words, and there are only words.

ACKNOWLEDGEMENT

I would like to extend my eternal gratitude to my Mum, Vicki Griffin. Without her everything, I never would have picked up a pen to write.

My son Rhett, who has to listen to me prattle and backtrack, doubt myself and be full of myself. He has never let me down.

Alyce and Mel L. Who always encouraged me to push past my limits and just write.

My siblings, Allan, Jessica and Jeremy. They never stopped believing in me.

Ms Jo McNamee. The best English teacher in the world.

Finally, to the one and only man who broke my heart xx

PREFACE

Of Grave Dirt and Stardust is a poetry collection which encompasses the authors highs and lows in all subjects across her Universe.
While there is no single theme, all her words are connected to her very core.

Within a Dream

I dreamt of you within the midnight hours.
So vivid I could almost feel you there.
You could hear my heart beating out of control,
you were so close I could almost smell your hair.

You held my gaze so steady, your hands upon
my face.
You were so real; I could almost kiss your lips.
You growled my name in low tones-words never
seemed to matter.
It was almost too perfect, so real, vivid and true.

I was almost close enough to love you,
then I awoke to the emptiness without you. . .

This Darkness

This darkness,
No longer holds me at an arm's length.
Now, it wraps me within its folds,

This darkness.

It comforts every single inch of me.
For every single second of the hour,
Has become an hour of desperate need.

This darkness.

Has become becoming.
The way it fills every space between every
moment.
No difference between joy or sorrow, pain or
hollow.
It consumes my entire entirety.

This Darkness.

Don't

Don't ever leave me alone,
back inside this place.
The dark is much too black,
with you leaving with such haste.

Don't wipe away my tears now,
when I don't deserve your touch.
When you kiss my mouth now,
the need becomes much too much.

Don't touch my skin with your caress,
so gentle yet so deep.
My soul is heavy with distress,
when you leave you leave me weak.

Don't plead with me for forgiveness,
when I know you've done no wrong.
I don't need your many reasons,
so don't tell me to be strong.

Don't leave me all alone again.
Back inside this place.
The dark is so much too dark now.
Don't leave me with such haste...

Click Like

Those notifications appearing on my screen,
The rush of endorphins reign supreme,
Knowing that validation from strangers across
the planet,
Nothing in real life can beat this feeling, can it?

Post after post it worsens and worsens,
Compare and comparisons with all other
persons.
Not good enough or pretty enough it seems,
This wide world web tangles all dreams.

Like like love love laugh react,
Down the social media rabbit hole,
We fall...
There's no coming back.

Little Things.

Sometimes my mind wanders & it whispers out
your name
Echoes of tender words spoken softly through
the night,
every moment made your eyes shine so bright
That was so long ago I long to hold you near...
Your name remains carved on my heart
forevermore awash with the tears.
Emotions so raw, twist like a blade.
Long for promises to become unmade.
For better or worse 'til death do us part.
For when you disappeared you tore me apart.

Embrace

Standing out in any crowd
Isn't at all hard for you to do.
But when your eyes fell upon mine,
We were only two.

I placed my heart within your hand,
The moment you breathed my name.
This sweet disconnection to reality,
Our Worlds will never be the same.

Deafened by my heartbeat,
With each step towards you I take.
As your lips draw towards mine,
The ground begins to shake.

I barely seem to know you,
Yet my blood begins to race.
The closer still I stand to you,
The warmer your eyes embrace.

I don't know if this is forever,
Or only just one night.
The moment your eyes lock on mine,
Everything just seems right.

Everything love used to be,
Every smile,
Every breath,
Every tear,
Twists the rules a little more,
The moment I sense you near.

For You

I tried so very hard for you,
to be perfect,
kind,
be true.

I even pushed my whole world aside,
Now it's gone.
You're gone...
I don't know what to do.

Whether I want to
or not,
I have to keep this mask
on my face.

Even when my World keeps
on crushing me,
I can never find enough
breathing space.

It must have hurt
this much before.
Pain's a memory
that fades away...

Yet my heart still
twists now
in pain.

You

Were

Meant

To

Stay...

Letting On

I will not let you go now.
I am not sure that was right.
I cannot let you go now.
Not with how I ache all through the night.

Your name is on my lips now.
You burn throughout my soul.
Your name etched on my heart now.
That burn is what makes me whole.

I dare not believe in you now.
When you promise that you will stay.
I should not believe in you now.
My heart is already feeling the fray.

I will not let you in now.
When you know what is inside my heart.
I cannot let you in now.
Your love is what is tearing me apart.

Again

You told me you loved me.
Then you were gone.
my grief came.
It lasted too long.

Then you were there,
with your smug apologies.
So now you can see...
The only fool is me...

Hollowed Out

I shed that skin today,
the skin that made me cry.
Then I left it behind,
That skin that made me say goodbye.

Over-absorbed, understand not,
This is the skin that changed me,
This is the skin which grew so hard.
I felt nothing.

And even now I feel nothing.
I feel nothing!

Empty.
 Hollow.

Numb.

Within this skin no life exists.
I cannot be her anymore,
She was never good enough anyway.
Maybe this skin will be whole again someday.

Oceans Apart

My heart beats ever so gently,
Since you have been away,
My mind still argues, finding ways,
that I could have made you stay.

When our souls first met,
It was so intense so fast.
Now I can't even begin to grasp,
That 'we' now live within our past.

Everytime I close my eyes,
My whole world begins to ache.
Dreams so vividly tormenting,
Yet still I do not wish to wake.

You belong to me, my love,
As the ocean meets the shore.
Still it matters not what I feel,
As I no longer belong to you anymore.

Shadows

Sadly you are just a reflection of somebody I
used to know,
We didn't even get the chance to beg each other
not to go.

Yet you linger like a dream I was never able to
touch,
We don't really have the right to miss each other
so much.

Now we are fading shadows destined to
disappear,
twilight falls around us hiding unshed tears...

Yesterday

It seems like only yesterday,
I was awaking with you by my side,
Yet every day since yesterday,
All I want to do is hide.

'We' didn't appear to be very special,
Did you know you made me smile?
And ever since that yesterday,
I have not smiled the same way in a little while.

When you said goodbye to me,
I sat on the stairs and began to cry.
Reliving every little yesterday,
Makes my heart slowly die.

It seems like only yesterday,
You held my soul within your hand.
And every hour since yesterday,
I still try to make my heart understand.

Yearn

So this begins.
This yearn for you.
Which turns me.
Inside out.

It always begins the same.
With your name dripping from my lips.
An echo of my heartbeat.
A sigh in the early hours.

You're
No
Longer
There.

I'll
Pretend
Not
To care.

So
I
Yearn
For you.

Muse

No emotion has ever been so painful so
powerful,
That it becomes even worse when you realise,
This pathos is your own creation.
Your very own misery.

There seems to be three personas within your
soul.
The first is the one so down, so low.
She cannot even raise her chin to meet her eyes
reflection.
The second she gazes down,
With a steady look of disappointment, in her sad
eyes.

Finally, there is you.
Unable to comprehend what to do.
How to rectify the situation.
Who doesn't know what will stop the steady
flow of tears,
rolling down your face.

The tears that scald the very core of you.
Only to know when you awake the next day and
the next,
It will feel so much worse and exactly the same.

Flowers

You always asked for flowers,
To place gently in your vase,
There was a beauty to their delicateness,
You especially loved roses.

 You always asked for flowers,
The way they made you smile,
You could fill a room with blooms,
They tended your soul.

You always asked for flowers,
They never let you down,
Even when the wilted,
You still saw the beauty.

You always asked for flowers.

Rhett

It was only yesterday,
Than I held you in the crook of my elbow,
Now your height towers over me,
You grew too quickly.

Fifteen years passed like lightening,
I barely had time to appreciate it,
Those chubby hands,
Grabbing my face for kisses.

Now you are the one holding me up,
Making sure I am okay,
I can't believe how amazing you are,
How perfection keeps getting better.

I made you and you made me the person I am
today,
You were the missing piece,
I never knew I needed,
You made me whole.

Grief

Is death better than grief?
I'd rather to not exist at all,
than to feel existence all at once.

It feels like if I breathe to deeply,
I will break into pieces,
If I breathe to shallowly,
My insides will shatter.

This grief will never go away,
Each day it grows heavier still,
I just have to become stronger,
So I can carry the weight of it suffocating me.

I drown in this pool of heartache,
There is no energy to cry for help,
I will just sink into its all consuming depths,
I will stay there and mourn all that I have lost.

Windows

21

Those eyes,
That catch me when I fall.
Within those eyes,
It's like we hardly exist at all.

I dare not look away,
From those eyes that behold my capture,
Deeply lost within reflected rapture.

Those eyes.
Those eyes.
Those eyes!

I cannot. I dare not look away.
Within only those eyes,
Is where my heart chooses to stay.

Too Late

I never thought I would miss the chance,
To tell you how I felt.
I thought we had a little longer,
To hold on to each other a little stronger.

You nurtured me from seed to fully grown,
I never knew a person could be my whole home.
Your absence is a pain I have never known,
It makes me wish, that I was not fully grown.

I hope you knew how much I loved you.

Skin

I find comfort in this skin,
There was a time I didn't even let myself in.
Now I have found a niche to rest,
All I ever have to do is my best.

No standards to live up to,
No expectations to let down.
In solitary was the last place,
I expected to be found.

This skin fits perfectly.
I wish I had found it earlier.
It feels nice to belong.
Even if it is only my skin.